The Civil War

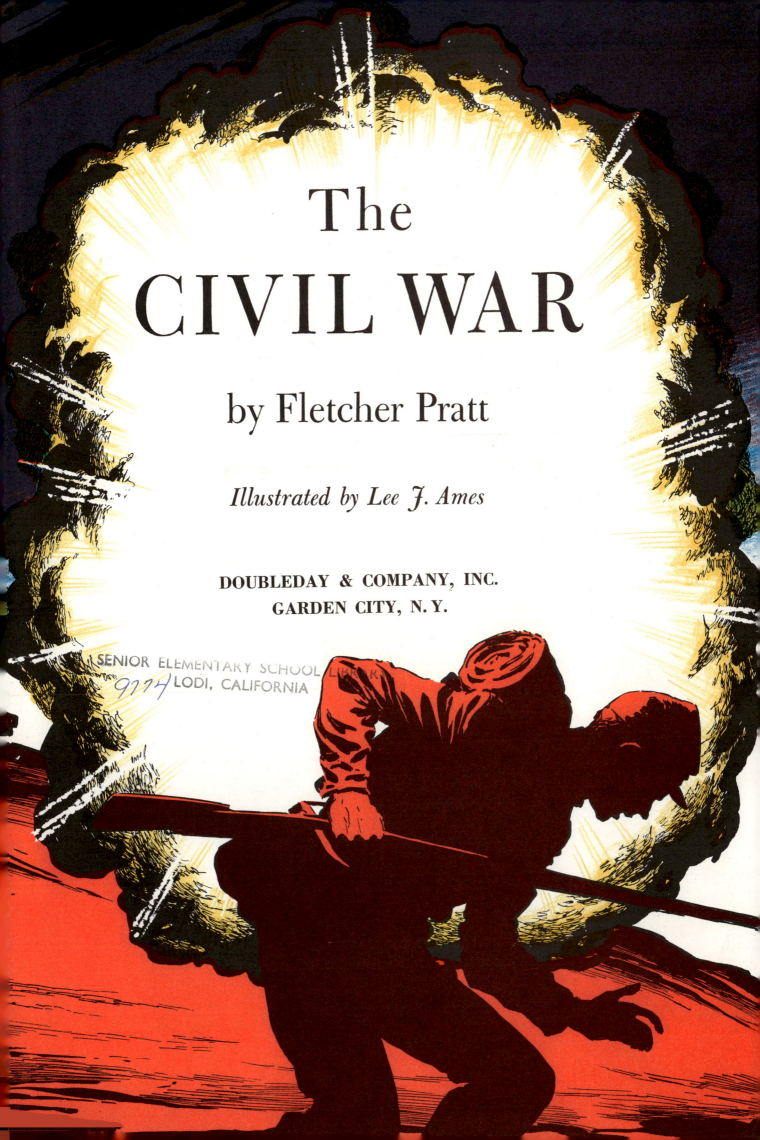

The
CIVIL WAR

by Fletcher Pratt

Illustrated by Lee J. Ames

DOUBLEDAY & COMPANY, INC.
GARDEN CITY, N. Y.

Library of Congress Catalog Card Number: 55-9718

Contents

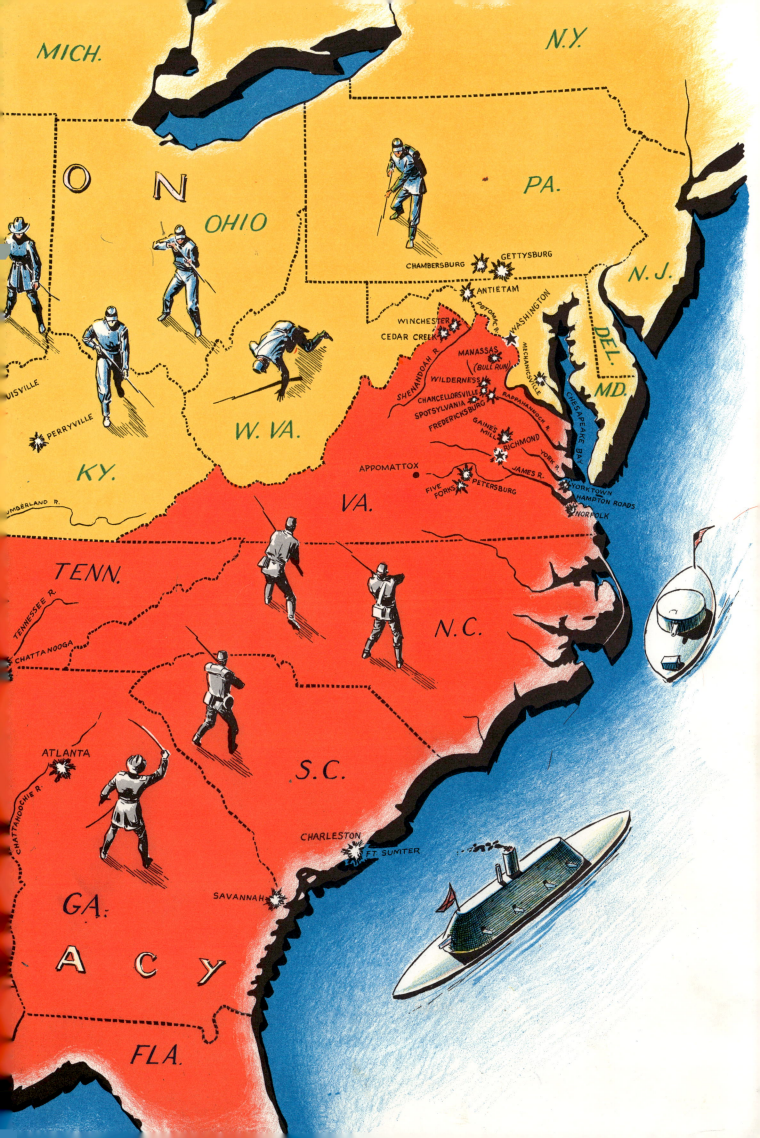

The Civil War

Part One

THE BEGINNING OF THE WAR
[1860–1861]

Before the Civil War the Negroes in the South were slaves. Many people in the North thought this was wrong and formed a party to prevent the spread of slavery. When this party elected Abraham Lincoln President of the United States, people in the slave states became very angry. They thought Lincoln and his party were going to take their slaves away, and then they would be unable to grow cotton, which was almost the only thing their farms produced.

The same Southerners who held the slaves also believed that each state had the right to leave the Union whenever it wished. After Lincoln was elected, people in seven of these states held conventions. They decided they would no longer stay in the Union, and set up a new nation which they called the Confederate States of America. Jefferson Davis was elected President.

South Carolina was one of the states that left the Union, or seceded. On an island in the harbor of Charleston, South Carolina, stood a big stone fort named Fort Sumter. President Lincoln would not let this fort be given up to the new government. He said it belonged to the United States and no state had a right to leave the Union and take things that belonged to the whole country.

The Confederates set up batteries on the shore all around the fort. They knew that if they opened fire on the American flag it would start a war, but they were quite willing. There were eight other slave states still in the Union. The Confederates thought that if the war began all eight would join them. They would then have Washington for their capital, and the new nation would easily become independent. So they fired on the fort. The day they began, all the ladies of Charleston came out in parasols and wide skirts and waved at the gunners.

Fort Sumter soon ran out of ammunition and was forced to surrender, and the war had started. But the Confederates were disappointed. Four of the slave states joined them, and they made Richmond their capital, but Maryland did not, so they did not get Washington. They had not expected the North to be willing to fight, either. But when people heard the flag had been fired on, meetings were held all over the North and men began enlisting to put down the rebellion. In Boston the bells rang all day long to call people out, and in

New York thousands of people turned out and cheered for more than two hours as the first regiment went south.

But when these new soldiers reached the camps that soon sprang up around Washington, they quickly found things very different. Many of them did not even know how to load a gun and few of them knew how to cook or had ever spent a night outdoors. They had to learn how to march in step, and they did not understand the orders their officers gave them. When two regiments met at a crossroads, nobody understood how to get one past the other, and there would be an argument.

THE BATTLE OF BULL RUN
[July 1861]

GENERAL IRVIN McDOWELL, who commanded this army, wanted to drill it more, but all the Northern newspapers insisted that he march to Richmond at once, and he had to try. He started on a hot day in July. It was more like a holiday than a march. Many Congressmen and ladies in carriages came along, and whenever the men felt like it, they dropped out to pick berries or get water from one of the streams.

At last they found the Confederates drawn up on a hill behind a stream named Bull Run, and attacked them. In the beginning everything went well for the Union army. Part of the Confederates were driven from the field, and it seemed that the rest must soon follow. But those who were left were commanded by General Thomas J. Jackson. One of the Confederate officers rode down the line, shouting, "There stands Jackson like a stone wall!" This was how this famous general got his name.

The Union soldiers had become very disorderly in the smoke and heat. Many of them had lost their officers and regiments and were simply wandering around. They could not advance against Jackson's stone wall. Just at this moment another small Confederate army appeared behind the Union troops. Some of them began to run and soon the whole army was flying back toward Washington as fast as it could. It was raining hard when the men reached the city and many of them wandered around in the streets all night.

This was the Battle of Bull Run. Everyone in the South now thought they were going to win the war easily and quickly. People in the North were sad, but now they saw it would not be enough to give some men guns and tell them to go to Richmond. President Lincoln called on General George B. McClellan to come to Washington and drill the men there until they were soldiers.

General McClellan was quite a young man, who had shown he was very good at drilling troops in Ohio. The people of western Virginia did not wish to leave the Union when their state seceded. They had formed the new state of West Virginia and asked McClellan for help. His men were better trained than the Confederates and easily beat them in two small battles. This was how West Virginia became a state and McClellan was called to Washington.

During the rest of the year there was hardly any fighting on land. On the Union side camps were set up all across the country, where the men marched and practiced with their guns, while the women made uniforms and flags. The Confederates thought they could win the war merely by keeping what they had. They set up forts along the coast and on the Mississippi and other rivers to keep ships from going up or down. Two important forts, named Henry and Donelson, were built to hold the Tennessee and Cumberland rivers. On both sides river steamers were rebuilt into gunboats.

THE BLOCKADE

THE CONFEDERATES had no navy on the ocean and the few ships belonging to the Union government were scattered all over the world when the war began. Nevertheless President Lincoln declared all the coasts of the Confederacy under blockade. This meant that any ship belonging to any nation could be captured if it tried to go in or out. The Confederates did not take this seriously. A blockade does not count unless there is a warship at the mouth of a harbor. They knew that the Union had nowhere near enough ships to close all their harbors, and they thought English ships would bring them the things they needed.

But the Union began buying up every kind of ship that would carry a gun and sending it to the Southern harbors. Even side-wheel ferryboats from New York and Boston were given small guns and sent to join the blockaders. They were not intended for such work and their decks were so weak that they sometimes broke when the guns were fired, but they did close the harbors.

At the same time all the shipyards in the North began building new warships. One group of them were called "ninety-day gunboats" because twenty-three of them were built in three months from the time work began. Before the end of the year the Union had added over a hundred and fifty ships to its navy. The English ships did not come.

The blockade was one of the most important things in the war. It did not make much noise and it was very hard work, because no matter how cold and wet it was or how fiercely the wind blew the blockaders had to stay where they were. But the blockade hurt the Confederacy badly because there were almost no factories in the South. The Confederates soon found it hard to get guns and ammunition. Things like needles, matches, paper, medicines, dishes for cooking, wagon wheels, and even blankets became very scarce.

To make matters worse the Union soon sent expeditions to capture some of the sandy islands off the Southern coast. These were defended by forts, but they were no match for the heavy guns of seagoing warships. After this, Union

ships began to run up the rivers behind the islands, breaking bridges and railroads and doing plenty of damage. The ferryboats were especially good at this because they had rudders at both ends and did not have to turn around. So the Union built a number of strange-looking warships called "double-enders," which did not have to turn around either.

THE FIRST BATTLE OF IRON SHIPS
[*March 8–9, 1862*]

IT WAS to break the blockade that the Confederates built their famous ironclad, the *Virginia*. She is often called the *Merrimack*, because that had been her name when she was a frigate in the U. S. Navy. When Virginia seceded, this ship was at Norfolk, but her engines were not working, so she was burned to keep her out of the hands of the Confederates. But she only burned down to the second deck before sinking. The Confederates raised her. On the deck that was left they built a box that looked like the roof of a barn, covered with iron plates four inches thick. Inside the box were ten of the biggest guns they could find. Her bow was fitted with a strong iron ram.

In March she came down into Hampton Roads. This was an important Union base, with a fort on the shore. Inside the Roads were the sailing frigate *Congress* of 44 guns and the sloop *Cumberland* of 28. They were built of wood, like nearly all other warships at that time. The *Virginia* attacked the *Cumberland* first. The Union ship fired as fast as she could but her solid shot simply bounced off the iron armor, while shells broke in pieces against it. The *Virginia* fired shells which killed many of the *Cumberland's* crew, then rammed her and tore a great hole in her side. She sank until only her flag remained above water. Now the *Virginia* turned on the *Congress* and fired shells into her until she was burning from end to end.

By this time it was growing dark. The big steam frigate *Minnesota* had come into the Roads to join the battle, but she had run aground. The people of the *Virginia* thought they could easily finish her and the rest of the blockading fleet the next day.

This was what everyone else expected, but when the *Virginia* came out the next morning there was something between her and the *Minnesota*. It looked like a cheesebox on a raft and it was several minutes before anyone on the *Virginia* realized it was a ship, one of the strangest ever built. It was the *Monitor*, invented by a Swedish engineer named John Ericsson, who came to this country to build ships. The cheesebox was a strong iron turret that turned round and round and held two heavy guns. The raft, nearly level with the water, had iron armor on top and around the edges. John Ericsson had made drawings and a model of this strange ship several years before, but people thought he was crazy and paid no attention.

But when the Confederates began building the *Virginia*, it was clear that the Union navy would soon have to have iron ships too. President Lincoln looked at the drawings for the *Monitor* and said she should be built. John Ericsson had to do everything in a great hurry, and most of the parts of his strange warship he had to invent for himself. The machinery he invented to hoist heavy shot up into the turret was the beginning of most of the elevators in modern buildings.

As the *Virginia* approached the *Minnesota*, the little *Monitor* steamed in between. The Confederate ship fired all her guns, but the shot simply bounced off the *Monitor's* armor in a cloud of sparks. Then the turret turned and two heavy shot banged into the *Virginia's* side. They did not go through, but they broke some of the iron armor, and the Confederates knew they had a fight on their hands.

For several hours the two ships circled around each other, firing hard. The *Virginia* tried to ram the *Monitor*, but the little ship's iron side was too strong. She tried to shoot at the portholes but the turret turned too fast. Finally the *Virginia* lost her smokestack and was badly battered. Her guns stopped shooting.

"Why are you no longer firing?" her captain asked.

"Because I can do her as much damage by snapping my fingers every two minutes," answered the gunner.

After this the *Virginia* turned and went back to Norfolk. When a Union army landed nearby she had to be blown up. John Ericsson built many more monitors and they helped greatly in making the blockade tight.

GENERAL McCLELLAN TRIES TO TAKE RICHMOND
[April–June 1862]

GENERAL McCLELLAN called his army the Army of the Potomac. He was fond of holding parades and his men all liked him because he treated them well. But all fall and winter long he did nothing but drill and hold more parades. It became clear he was not very anxious to fight and in the spring President Lincoln told him he would have to do something.

But McClellan did not march against the Confederate army at Manassas where Bull Run was fought. Instead he put his men on ships and took them to the mouth of the James River near Norfolk. He intended to march up the peninsula between this river and the York and take Richmond. He thought that if the Confederates lost their capital they would give up. Meanwhile he could get supplies by water up the York River, and the Confederates could not interfere because they had no navy.

But when McClellan's army got as far up the peninsula as Yorktown it found some forts. McClellan sent for big guns to besiege the forts while the army sat down and camped. There was not much shooting and everybody was having a good time. For over a month the guns banged away. Then one morning the soldiers noticed that the Confederates were not shooting back. They found the forts were empty and most of the guns in them had been painted wood to fool McClellan.

Of course the month McClellan spent at Yorktown gave the Confederates time to build new forts, close around Richmond. McClellan moved his army up to them, so close he could hear the churchbells in the city ring. But then he simply waited. He thought the Confederates had more men than he did, while really it was the other way around.

In Richmond people were not happy. It was hard for anyone to find a place to live because there were so many soldiers and wives of soldiers. Because of the blockade coffee and tea cost ten dollars a pound, and it was hard to find ordinary things to eat. When holes were worn in clothes they had to be patched, because the South had no factories to make cloth.

General Joe Johnston commanded the Confederate army in Richmond. He decided things could not go on like this and something must be done to to drive McClellan away from the city. Part of McClellan's men were on one side of the Chickahominy River and part on the other. If one of these parts were attacked, the other might have trouble getting across the river in time to help. So Johnston brought nearly all his men to the south bank of the river and attacked. This was the first real battle for both armies, and the woods were thick, so that men stumbled around among the trees and fired at each other without knowing quite what they were doing. At first the Confederates were

successful, but then they became scattered and were driven back. All night long lines of ambulances carried wounded men into Richmond, and the schools and churches were used as hospitals while women made bandages.

One of the wounded was General Johnston. The command of the Confederate army was now given to General Robert E. Lee, which turned out well for the Confederacy, because he was one of the greatest soldiers in American history.

GENERAL LEE AND STONEWALL JACKSON
[June 1862]

As LEE had fewer men than McClellan he had to make a clever plan to drive the Union army away from Richmond. There was a small army in the Shenandoah Valley under Stonewall Jackson. Lee sent part of his men to Jackson and told him to do something that would worry the Union government, so it would not send McClellan any more men.

Jackson was a very good choice. He marched his men so far and so fast that they called themselves the "foot cavalry." He himself hardly ever seemed to sleep, and when he looked at a piece of country, he knew exactly where every man and gun should be placed in a battle. His men always expected to win.

There were two different Union armies in the Shenandoah Valley. Jackson had more men than either one alone. He attacked one of them and beat it, then marched so fast that the other Union army did not know he was coming, so he beat that too. Everyone in Washington was angry, and frightened because they thought Jackson might cross the Potomac and come to the capital. President Lincoln sent troops from all directions to catch Jackson. Some of them had been intended to join McClellan's army but now he would never get them. Jackson beat each of the separate armies in turn, and then hurried to join Lee. The Union troops following him wore out their shoes and the wagons carrying their food and ammunition could not keep up, so they had to stop.

19

THE SEVEN DAYS' BATTLES
[June–July 1862]

Now Lee was ready to drive McClellan away from Richmond. The Confederate cavalry were commanded by General Jeb Stuart, a gay general with a big black beard, who always wore plumes in his hat and begged pretty girls for roses. The first step in Lee's plan was to send Stuart around McClellan's army to get between him and his storehouses on the York River. Stuart's men rode right around McClellan's army without being stopped. They burned $7,000,000 worth of supplies and ran all McClellan's railroad trains into the river.

Now McClellan would quickly have to move his army to a place where he could get supplies. But Lee did not intend that he should get away. He moved most of the Confederates to the north bank of the Chickahominy and attacked the part of the Union army there. Jackson was supposed to get around behind them and capture them all. This was called the Battle of Gaines' Mill. It was fought on a day so hot that the men could hardly bear to touch their rifles. The Union troops were driven back, but their artillery turned out to be very good, and at every place where there was open ground, the fire of the guns held up the Confederates. In addition, Jackson was late for some reason no one was ever able to understand, and did not get behind the Union lines. The Army of the Potomac lost a good many men, but all of it gathered on the south bank during the night.

But McClellan was not out of trouble yet. He now had to march to the James River to get supplies from ships. The way led along narrow roads through great swamps filled with trees, so the army had to be strung out in long, narrow columns on the roads. Of course Lee knew this. He brought his men south of the Chickahominy and sent them out from Richmond to cut the columns in two, while Jackson attacked them from behind. All through the next week there were battles, battles, battles in the gloomy swamps, with smoke drifting through the trees and long lines of wagons carrying the wounded. All the guns

of the Civil War made a great deal of smoke when they were fired, and in these battles it often became difficult to see where you were going.

Lee never did succeed in breaking through the columns. When the armies reached the James he had lost more men than McClellan. But the Union army was now shut up in its camp on the river and McClellan was further from taking Richmond than ever. The men were unhappy and so was President Lincoln. People kept urging him to give the army to someone else, but no one could suggest anyone who would be better.

HOW GENERAL GRANT GOT HIS NAME
[February 1862]

A STOCKY GENERAL named U. S. Grant was placed in charge of the troops in western Kentucky. He did not talk much and he was usually seen smoking a big cigar, but he had his own way of doing things. When one of his officers ate nearly all the food in a woman's house, Grant sent him back with 100 cavalry to eat the rest and pay for all the food.

Grant often went to St. Louis. While he was there he saw some of the gunboats the navy men had gone there to build. They had flat bottoms and square ends that made them look like turtles. At the front and part of the way along the sides they had iron armor but it was not very thick. But when Grant saw them, he thought they could be used to attack the Confederate forts on the rivers in front while troops closed on them from behind.

General H. W. Halleck was in command of all the Union armies in the West. He was called "Old Brains" because he knew so much about the history of war, but he did not want to let Grant go because no one had ever done such a thing before. But he finally agreed to let Grant try it against Fort Henry, which was the weakest. Early in February, Grant started up the Tennessee River. The troops were landed to march on the fort while the gunboats pushed on ahead. They shot so fast and hard that when the soldiers reached the fort the Confederates had surrendered.

As Grant had taken this fort without any fighting, he cut the telegraph wires to keep Halleck from calling him back, and marched across country for Fort Donelson on the Cumberland River. It became quite warm during the march and many of the soldiers threw away their overcoats and blankets. But when they reached the fort it began to rain and freeze. The men could not even build fires because the Confederates would shoot at them. All they had to eat were the big biscuits called "hardtack."

Next morning the gunboats came up the river and began to shoot. Fort Donelson had a large army inside and heavy guns, high on the hills. The shells from these guns plunged through the tops of the gunboats, where they had no armor, and exploded in the boilers, filling them with scalding steam. Soon all the gunboats were disabled and drifting down the river. Grant rode down after them to see if anything could be done. While he was on the way he heard the sound of guns behind him and hurried back.

He found the Confederates had attacked his lines and nearly broken through in one place. The general there wanted help. Just then some prisoners were led past. Grant noticed their knapsacks were very full and asked to see one of them. It was full of bread and cooked bacon.

"These men have rations for a march, not a fight," said Grant. "They are trying to escape." Instead of sending help to the general who had asked for it, Grant ordered all his men to attack. They took so much of the fort that the rest would never be able to hold out, and the Confederate general sent a messenger with a white flag to ask what terms Grant would give. Grant said his only terms were unconditional surrender, and the Confederates surrendered their whole army of 21,000 men. After this he was known as "Unconditional Surrender" Grant because the initials matched those of his name.

THE BATTLE OF SHILOH
[April 6–7, 1862]

GRANT now began to advance up the Tennessee River and Halleck ordered another army under General Don Carlos Buell from eastern Kentucky to help him. One night Grant's army camped on the west bank at a landing near Shiloh Church, in rough open woods. Not many guards were posted and they were not far out because everyone thought the Confederates were some distance away.

This was a mistake. General Albert Sidney Johnston had brought the whole Confederate Western army up very quietly and it was just outside Grant's camp. While the Union soldiers were eating their breakfast the Confederates gave a tremendous yell and charged.

At first the Confederates drove the Union troops before them and captured a number of men. But these were new soldiers who did not know much about keeping together in battle. In the smoke, among the trees and gullies, little groups would get separated and fight with other little groups on the Union side for a patch of woods or a hill. No one in America had ever seen such fighting. There were trees with every leaf taken off by bullets and fields where you could walk from one side to the other across the bodies of dead men on the ground. Grant rode everywhere, trying to straighten his lines. His horse was killed under him and four bullets went through his clothes. The

Confederate general was killed, but by nightfall the Union army had been driven back until it was just barely holding the steamboat landing. If the Confederates took it in the morning the army would be lost. Men on both sides lay on the ground with their guns beside them and tried to get some sleep, but they did not get much because every now and then the artillery would begin to bang again.

At two o'clock in the morning Buell's men began to arrive on boats and paraded into Grant's lines under torchlight. As soon as it was light enough to see, the shooting began again on both sides. But with all Buell's men on the field it was now the turn of the Union army to move forward. The fighting was just as hard as on the first day, but now there were just too many Union troops and too many Union guns. The Confederates were driven back and back, and finally had to give up and retreat into Mississippi.

Each side lost 10,000 men at Shiloh, which took place before the battles between Lee and McClellan. Before Shiloh, everyone thought that one big battle would end the war. Shiloh made it certain that neither side would give up easily. In the North they began offering money to anyone who would become a soldier. In the South they passed a law that every young man had to serve as a soldier. Huge cannon factories were set up at Pittsburgh and in the Confederacy they began building factories to make iron.

CLEARING THE RIVER FORTS
[March 1862]

ONE of the most important Confederate forts on the Mississippi was at Island No. 10. It stood on a point just where the river turns back north for a short distance before going south again at the Tennessee-Kentucky line. Behind it there were deep swamps that kept anyone from getting at it on the land side. An army that marched down the opposite side would also run into swamps there and could only get its supplies from ships coming down the river. But the fort at Island No. 10 kept the ships from going down.

General John Pope commanded the Union army that was trying to go down the river toward Memphis. He could not figure out how to get past that fort. Finally, the navy dug a canal through the point of land behind Island No. 10. This was quite a job, since the men had to work in water up to their waists, sawing the tough trees, while soldiers in the treetops kept off the Confederates who crawled through the swamps to shoot at them.

Now General Pope could send his men through the canal in small boats and supplies could follow them in the same way. But the men had to land on the western side of the river because the Confederates had batteries all along the east bank, so this was not much better. They needed an ironclad gunboat to do something about the batteries. Henry Walke, captain of the gunboat *Carondelet*, agreed to try to take his ship past Island No. 10, although its guns were so heavy that a single shot would sink his ship.

He chose a dark, cloudy night, and got halfway past the fort without being seen. But then the soot in his smokestacks caught fire and made the whole river bright as day. At the same moment a thunderstorm began, with lightning flashing all around while the guns of the fort boomed. But they did not hit the *Carondelet*, and when she got below Island No. 10 she easily finished off the light batteries on the east bank. Now General Pope's soldiers crossed over and Island No. 10 was cut off, so it had to surrender with 7000 men.

General Pope now wished to go on to Memphis, but his supplies and most of his men still had to come down the river. At Memphis the Confederates had a fleet of eight ships. They had no plates to make iron armor for these ships so they piled cotton bales around their sides. These ships had light guns and strong iron prows to ram the enemy. Once they sank one of the Union ironclads.

Just as the four Union gunboats were ready to go down the river they were joined by four odd ships, built by Colonel Charles Ellet of the army. They were rams, too, but as Ellet wanted them to be very fast he gave them no guns at all to carry. When the Union gunboats came down the river everyone in Memphis went out on the bluffs with picnic lunches to watch the battle.

The four armored gunboats came first. They made so much smoke from their funnels and their guns that none of the Confederates saw Ellet's rams behind them. The Confederate rams spread out to attack the gunboats from all sides at once. Some of them were badly damaged by the heavy guns of the Union fleet. At this moment Ellet's rams dashed through the Union fleet. One of them cut a Confederate ship in half, and another moved so fast that two Confederates rammed each other trying to get at her. The heavy guns of the Union ships tore the Confederates to pieces, and they turned to run away down the river, but the rams caught them and all but one were sunk. The picnickers on the bluffs sadly went home, and General Pope took Memphis the next day.

FARRAGUT AT NEW ORLEANS
[April 18–28, 1862]

NEW ORLEANS was the largest city in the Confederacy. On the river below it lay two large forts, and there was a small fleet of river ships with light guns to help them. The Confederates were building two huge ironclads at New Orleans. The Union navy had only wooden ships to blockade the mouth of the river, so they decided New Orleans must be taken before the Confederate ironclads were finished. A fleet was sent out under D. G. Farragut who, although he was an old man with long white hair, used to turn somersaults on deck every morning.

He had twenty mortar schooners, each with one big, very short gun between its masts, throwing shells almost straight up into the air. These were placed behind a bend in the river, with branches tied to their masts to keep the Confederates from seeing them. For several days they fired a shell a minute into the forts, but they were not much damaged. One of the Confederate ironclads was so nearly finished that she came down to the forts and anchored to have her engines repaired. Farragut decided he would have to try to run past the forts with his fleet.

He had the sides of all his ships daubed with mud to make them harder to see and hung chains along them as a kind of armor. As these were oceangoing ships, quite deep in the water, they had to go up one by one through the narrow channel in deep water. The start was made at two o'clock in the morning.

As the Union ships came around the bend below the forts huge bonfires sprang up on the banks and all the guns of the forts began firing. Some of Farragut's ships were damaged and driven back, but the big guns of the others drove the Confederates from their batteries. Just above the forts the Confederate river fleet charged through the smoke into Farragut's ships, helped by a surprise—huge fire rafts, fifty feet across, pushed by tugs.

One of these fire rafts was pushed against the side of Farragut's flagship. The rigging caught fire and the admiral's eyebrows were scorched off, while one of the Union ships was sunk. But the tug that pushed the fire raft was blown up and one by one the smaller Confederate ships were sunk or driven into the riverbank. At daybreak the tall Union ships reached New Orleans. Crowds came to the docks, shaking their fists at the ships and setting fire to bales of cotton which they threw in the river.

The Union sailors only patted their big guns and grinned. New Orleans was taken, and since the forts were now cut off from supplies, they had to surrender too. New Orleans was the only city in the Confederacy where they could coin money. After it was taken everyone had to use postage stamps to buy things.

LEE AND JACKSON AGAIN
[August 1862]

AFTER McClellan and his army were shut up in their camp on the James River, President Lincoln called on the country to furnish more troops and they soon began to arrive in Washington. They did not march through the city with bands, like the regiments at the beginning of the war, but moved soberly down the streets, which were just then being torn up so new streetcar tracks could be laid. These new men, with some from McClellan's army, were made into a new army and were sent down into Virginia along the Blue Ridge Mountains to approach Richmond from that direction.

General John Pope was brought from the West to command this army. As soon as Lee heard of this new army he hurried to meet it. Pope was expecting more troops to join him. Until they did, he fell back behind the Rappahannock River. It is very difficult for an army to cross a river when the enemy does not wish it unless the water is shallow enough to wade.

When Lee came up to the river he did a very bold thing. He sent Stonewall Jackson up the river and behind some mountains in a wide circle with nearly half his army. They marched all night and most of the day. Every hour they would rest for five minutes. They had to do their eating during this time and had no chance to make fires or coffee. Jackson kept riding along the line, saying, "Press on! Press on!" to make them go faster.

Behind the mountains Jackson turned and marched down to Manassas, where the Battle of Bull Run had been fought. Great storehouses for Pope's army had been built there. The Confederates took all the new clothes and shoes they wanted and had a delicious meal on the fine foods piled up for the Union army, then burned everything else.

When Pope heard that Jackson was between him and Washington he started back. At the same time Lee set off to follow Jackson. Of course some of Pope's men reached Manassas before the rest. They started a fight that lasted all day, but Jackson's men were behind a high railroad bank and easily beat them. The next day Lee joined Jackson. He came down on Pope's flank and behind him. The Union army was driven back to Washington in as much disorder as after the first battle at Manassas. Many people thought Lee would take Washington and piled all their furniture on wagons to leave the city.

But this was not what Lee had in mind. Most people in the South thought that because Maryland was a slave state it was really on their side, and if a Confederate army came, thousands of men would join it. So Lee crossed the Potomac into Maryland. He sent Stonewall Jackson with half his army in one direction, while he took another. But he was very disappointed in Maryland. Instead of cheering and joining him, people simply closed their doors and stared from the windows at the ragged, dirty soldiers. They did not even want to sell food to the Confederates.

THE BATTLE OF ANTIETAM
[September 17, 1862]

LEE sent a letter to Jackson telling him about his plans. The letter fell out of the messenger's pocket, and a Union soldier found it. General McClellan had been called back to Washington after Pope was beaten. As soon as he saw Lee's letter, he knew that if he could get to Sharpsburg he would be between the two parts of Lee's army and could beat each in turn.

But McClellan could not make his men march like Jackson's. When he reached Sharpsburg he found Lee's whole army lined up behind Antietam Creek. The Confederates were still in a very bad position. They had the Potomac River behind them and if McClellan broke through their lines there was no place to go. So McClellan attacked and there was a terrible battle, lasting all day. Lee's lines were not broken, but he had to keep hurrying men from one spot to another and lost a great many of them. He had really been beaten this time, and his army was so badly hurt that it would be unable to do anything for a long while.

President Lincoln had been waiting for a victory to make an important announcement. Ever since the beginning of the war, the Confederacy had been trying to get help from France and England. While Lee's army was winning all the battles, it seemed likely that the Confederacy could never be beaten and France and England might interfere to stop the war. But now Lee had lost a battle and Lincoln issued the "Emancipation Proclamation." It set free all the slaves in states fighting against the government. France and England did not care to interfere in favor of a government that was fighting to keep men slaves against one that set them free.

McClellan followed Lee across the Potomac. But nearly two months went by and instead of fighting Lee's weaker army, McClellan only kept asking for more troops. Finally Lincoln grew indignant. He removed McClellan and gave the Army of the Potomac to General Ambrose Burnside, who wore the kind of whiskers that have been called "burnsides" ever since.

BRAGG IN KENTUCKY
[September–October 1862]

PRESIDENT LINCOLN called Halleck east to be his assistant. The Union armies that had fought at Shiloh under Grant and Buell were now separated. Grant was to start from Memphis, Tennessee, against Vicksburg, the great fortress by which the Confederates kept the Mississippi closed to Union ships, while Buell went east against Chattanooga, Tennessee. Chattanooga was very important

because all the railroad lines running through the mountains north and south, east and west, meet there.

The Confederate commander at Chattanooga was General Braxton Bragg. Buell's army was very slow in crossing Tennessee to come up with him, because his men had torn up all the railroad tracks. So Bragg decided to invade Kentucky, just as Lee was doing in Maryland about the same time. Kentucky was also a slave state. Bragg expected many thousands of men to join him, and took along wagonloads of arms for them.

When Bragg marched into Kentucky everyone in Louisville and Cincinnati was frightened. All the men turned out to dig trenches around the cities. The streetcars stopped running and the horses that drew them were taken for new regiments of cavalry. But Bragg did not go to the cities because Buell was following him so closely. For several weeks the two armies marched through the hot summer on dusty roads, and it was always hard to find a place with water, where they could camp for the night.

One afternoon the scouts for the two armies ran into each other near Perryville, Kentucky, while they were looking for water. They began to fight. Men on both sides heard the guns and hurried to where they were firing, and soon a battle was going on, with almost all the Confederate army and more than half the Union. The Union army was saved by a charge led by a young officer named Philip H. Sheridan. He was so small that they always called him "Little Phil."

The Battle of Perryville was very much like Antietam. After it was over Bragg retreated, back to Chattanooga. He had no more luck in getting the people of Kentucky to join him than Lee had in Maryland. But when Buell let Bragg get away, Lincoln gave the army to General William S. Rosecrans. Both Buell and McClellan could drill soldiers very well, but neither was anxious to fight battles, and Lincoln knew that the only way of saving the Union would be by fighting hard, even if many men were killed. People in the North often came to see him to ask him to stop the war, but this was what he always told them.

GRANT TRIES TO TAKE VICKSBURG
[August–December 1862]

THE FORTRESS at Vicksburg was set on bluffs two hundred feet high. Guns from ships could not reach the batteries on these bluffs. While the Confederates had Vicksburg they not only closed the river to the Union but could get men and supplies from the west.

Grant could not march down the east bank of the Mississippi against Vicksburg because the ground is swampy and covered with thick woods all the way down from Memphis. Far inland there is high, dry ground, leading down behind Vicksburg. Grant beat the Confederates in a couple of battles and tried to march down this ground. But when he had marched about sixty miles the Confederates sent their cavalry around behind him. They burned his depot of supplies and tore up the railroad behind him, so he had to go back to Memphis. Now Grant put his men on ships and took them down the river, opposite Vicksburg. They looked up at the forts on the bluffs, but they could not climb against the guns there.

Grant now tried digging a canal among the rivers in the swamps north of Vicksburg, but it could not be made deep enough for the gunboats. The Confederates had batteries on the riverbanks and Grant's transports could not go in without the help of the gunboats. Grant tried sending the gunboats up the Yazoo River, which cuts through the high ground near Vicksburg, but the Confederates cut down trees across the river and the gunboats could go no farther. He tried sending part of his men down the high ground behind Vicksburg to tempt the Confederates out of the fortress while others climbed the bluffs, but enough Confederates stayed to keep his men from climbing. In

all Grant tried seven different plans to reach the high ground behind Vicksburg, but the trouble was always that he could not get supplies to any men who got there.

The men were uncomfortable in their camps in the swamps across from Vicksburg. It rained a good deal of the time, there were thousands of mosquitoes, and many of the men became sick. They wrote letters home telling how badly things were going and their Congressmen went to ask Lincoln to remove Grant. The President listened to them, then walked to a window and stood looking out for a few minutes. Finally he turned around and said: "I can't spare that man. He fights." Grant went on trying to take Vicksburg.

FREDERICKSBURG
[December 1862]

THERE were two more big battles before the end of the year, but neither one of them decided anything. In Virginia General Burnside had the idea of marching the Army of the Potomac down the Rappahannock River and going straight to Richmond by way of Fredericksburg. Fredericksburg is on the low banks on the south side of the river, but all around it are steep hills with many stone walls.

Burnside expected to get up those hills before the Confederates knew what he was doing. But just as he started his march it began to rain. The men were up to their ankles in mud and the guns and wagons could hardly move at all. In addition, when Burnside reached Fredericksburg, he found there was no material to build bridges across the river. While he was waiting for it, the Confederates arrived and lined up behind the stone walls on the hills.

After the bridges were built, Burnside crossed into Fredericksburg and ordered his men to attack up the hills. All the men knew they could never make it, and many of them wrote their names on pieces of paper which they pinned to their coats, so their relatives could be notified when they were killed. All day the Union soldiers tried to climb those hills against the guns firing down at them. They lost 15,000 men and the Confederates hardly any.

After the battle the army was so discouraged that many men deserted and when Burnside went through the camps the soldiers hooted at him. Lincoln gave the Army of the Potomac to General Joseph Hooker, who was known as "Fighting Joe."

STONE RIVER
[December 31, 1862–January 2, 1863]

THE OTHER big battle was in central Tennessee, where Rosecrans marched out of Nashville and Bragg out of Chattanooga on the last day of the year. The armies met at Stone River. Each general intended to surprise the other by getting around his right wing, but Bragg started earlier in the morning. He surprised the Union right wing and drove nearly half the Union army away.

But then the Confederates came to a place called the Round Forest, which was held by General George H. Thomas. He was a big man with fuzzy whiskers, known as "Old Pap," who always put on his best uniform on the day of a battle so his men could see him. He rode along the line with the bullets flying around him, telling the men what to do and where to place the guns. The men cheered when they saw him and the Confederate attack was stopped.

Next day there was a little fighting, but both armies were tired and waiting for more bullets. During the night of the second day Rosecrans got many of his guns onto a high hill. On the morning of the third day he attacked in turn and with the help of the guns drove the Confederates from the field.

Part Two

TWO YEARS OF WAR

So STONE RIVER was a Union victory, but not one to be very proud of. More men were killed than at Shiloh and nothing was accomplished. At the end of 1862 things did not look very good for the Union. It had won all of Kentucky and most of Tennessee and Missouri beside the great city of New Orleans. But after two years of war the main armies in the east were still between Washington and Richmond, and nearly every time they came together the Confederates won the battle. The armies in Tennessee had battered away at each other without accomplishing anything, and Grant seemed unable to reach Vicksburg. On the ocean Confederate cruisers had burned many ships.

Plenty of people wanted the war to stop, even if it meant the end of the Union. Several of them were elected to Congress in 1862, and they blamed Lincoln for everything. It was growing harder to find men to be soldiers, and in every town there was some family who had lost someone. Prices were terribly high. Almost the only people never discouraged were Lincoln and Grant and the Union soldiers.

We know now that they were right. The Confederacy, which looked so strong, was growing weaker every day. Its railroads were wearing out and there were no new rails or cars. There was no way to sell the cotton the South produced and everyone was terribly poor. Clothes were wearing out and there was so little paper that newspapers printed only one or two sheets. Worst of all, it was even harder to find soldiers in the South than in the North. But still, hardly anybody believed the South would be beaten.

CHANCELLORSVILLE
[May 1–4, 1863]

THE FIRST THING "Fighting Joe" Hooker had to do was to make his army feel like fighting again. He allowed many of the men to go home for a short time during the winter. When they came back he drilled them hard but saw to it that they had plenty to eat and new weapons. In April, President Lincoln came down to visit the army in its camp across the Rappahannock from Fredericksburg. There was a big parade, and the men were singing as they marched past so Hooker knew they were feeling all right again.

He had twice as many men as Lee, but he also had the problem of getting across the river to fight the Confederates. Hooker made a good plan to do this. Some of his men crossed into Fredericksburg as though to attack the hills again. Some went farther up the river as though to get behind Lee. But most went still farther up and crossed into the wild woodland called The Wilderness, around Chancellorsville.

But Hooker never did think very fast, and when he got his men safely across the river, he could not think what to do next. So the army stopped while Lee came up to face it. There was a fight among the trees and hills, lasting nearly all day. By night neither side had gained much, but Hooker had so many more men that Lee knew he would have a hard time the next day. He sent Stonewall Jackson with nearly half the army by little-known paths through the Wilderness to get behind Hooker's army.

This was the most famous of all Jackson's marches. It started in the middle of the night. Next afternoon Jackson came out of the woods behind the Union right wing. The Union soldiers there who did not run away were quickly killed or captured, and Hooker's whole army began to crumple up like a piece of paper.

Hooker managed to get some men from various places and stop the Confederate advance, but by dark his army was badly cramped together. Stonewall Jackson planned to attack in the morning and cut the Union army off from the fords by which it crossed the river. Then it would have to surrender. He rode out in the night to find the best way. As he was coming back in the dark his own men mistook him for the enemy and fired. Jackson was mortally wounded.

Even without Jackson the Confederates drove the Union army back next morning until it had to cross the river. Hooker had lost a great many men and won nothing at all. When President Lincoln heard the news his face turned white and he almost fell down. When a Union army could not beat one half its size, it seemed as though the people who wanted to end the war might be right. New buildings had to be taken over for hospitals in Washington, and all over the North people were discouraged.

GETTYSBURG—THE GREATEST BATTLE
[June–July 1863]

THE CONFEDERATE leaders were now sure that Lee could never be beaten. They thought that if he invaded the North again and won a battle there the Union would be so discouraged that it would make peace. So Lee marched to the Shenandoah Valley and turned north. Soon he had crossed Maryland and was in Pennsylvania. His soldiers, who so often did not get enough to eat, had a fine time, getting everything they wanted.

The Union army turned north also, on the other side of the mountains, keeping between Lee and Washington. Everyone in the North was worried and men began digging trenches and planting guns around places like Pittsburgh and Philadelphia. To make matters more uncertain, General Hooker resigned just at this moment. Lincoln gave the army to General George Meade.

When large armies move, they have to take several roads going in more or less the same direction, and even so the head of a marching column may be as much as fifteen miles from the tail. For this reason it is very important to bring all the troops together before a battle is fought. When Lee heard that Meade was following him, he gave orders for his separate columns to meet at Gettysburg before the Union army could strike any one of them by itself.

There is a high hill west of Gettysburg with a school on it. Early on the morning of July 1, General John Reynolds climbed the clock tower of this school and saw the roads leading into Gettysburg from the west filled with a long column of Confederate soldiers, while more were coming from the north and east. He had only one corps but he knew that if the Confederates got together first the parts of the Union army would be beaten one by one. So he strung his men and guns out along the top of the hill and sent for the rest of the army to join him.

The first Confederates to arrive thought the Union men in front of them were only some home guards, who could be easily driven away. But they were surprised at how fast the Union men fired, and then a Union regiment stood up and charged them with the bayonet. It was the Wisconsin Iron Brigade, who wore special black hats. "Look at them black hats!" cried someone among the Confederates. "That's the Army of the Potomac!"

Now they had to spread out in a line opposite Reynolds' men and make it a regular battle. This took time, but there were so many more of the Confederates that they drove the Union line back, inch by inch. Reynolds was killed, and just about noon another Confederate column began to come down from the north, behind his line. But just at this moment another Union corps arrived. These were mostly Germans, the men who had run away at Chancellorsville. They were anxious to prove they were good soldiers after all, and charged and charged the Confederates as though they did not care what happened to themselves.

More and more Confederates kept coming and the Union force was slowly driven back through Gettysburg to a high hill called Cemetery Ridge. Here they found a number of guns and part of another corps that had just arrived. It was growing dark and General Lee's men had had a hard day of marching and fighting. So he decided to wait till morning before going on with the attack.

THE SECOND DAY
[July 2, 1863]

Cemetery Ridge is shaped like a fishhook, with the road down which Union troops were still coming at the eye end. Lee planned to make his main attack there to keep the rest of the Union army from getting together. There was a peach orchard on a low hill here and along it the Union line ran in an angle. Lee brought 160 cannon up against the peach orchard, and after they had shelled it, sent in a column of attack. The column broke through the angle and began to drive the Union troops back in both directions.

But just at this moment a new Union corps arrived. The men stepped right off the road and into battle across the fields without putting down their haversacks. The firing was so heavy that men could not stand in line, but had to lie on the ground behind trees and rocks and snake forward. Just as the Confederates began to gain, a Union officer named Warren noticed a hill called Little Round Top, which neither side had taken. He saw that if there were guns on this hill they could blow out the whole Union line.

Without asking anyone's permission Warren ordered the nearest troops to the top of the hill. They got there just in time to see Confederates coming up the other side, and a savage fight began, in which both sides used up all their ammunition and fought with clubbed muskets and knives and even stones. The Union soldiers won and Warren soon had guns on Little Round Top. Now still more Union troops began to arrive, and with the help of Warren's guns the Confederates were driven back into the twilight.

Up at the hook end of the Union line the Confederates also tried an attack toward evening, but Meade had placed his men so well that it was quickly beaten.

THE THIRD DAY—PICKETT'S CHARGE
[July 3, 1863]

All the same General Lee was sure he had struck the ends of the Union line such hard blows that its center must now be weak. He brought nearly all the guns in his army to this center to bombard the Union line, a mile away across the valley. This was to put the Union artillery out of action, and in fact it soon stopped firing. Then Lee sent General Pickett across the valley at the head of 15,000 men to break through the Union center on Cemetery Ridge.

They marched out in perfect lines across the grass and wheat fields, with their flags waving. There were so many it did not seem that anything could stop them. But as they reached the bottom of the valley and began to climb all the Union guns opened up again. They had only stopped firing to let them cool. They tore great gaps in Pickett's lines, but those who were left filled them up, gave a yell, and kept right on coming up the ridge. They reached the top and got right in among the Union guns. But there were now so few of them left that when the Union soldiers charged them with the bayonet they were driven out and down back across the valley.

General Lee had lost a third of his army. That night he began to retreat toward Virginia. The news of the victory at Gettysburg reached the Northern cities on the Fourth of July and made it a wonderful celebration. But before night there was another piece of great news. General Grant had taken Vicksburg and the whole army defending it.

GRANT AT VICKSBURG
[June–July 1863]

THE OTHER generals wanted Grant's army to go back to Memphis and start a new campaign, building a railroad line down the dry ground. But he had other ideas. He marched his men down the west bank of the Mississippi and crossed over at Bruinsburg. Then he started for Jackson, which was the railroad center connecting Vicksburg with the rest of the Confederacy.

He was on the high, dry ground behind Vicksburg at last, but all the other generals were frightened. Unarmored ships carrying supplies could not come down the river past the batteries and they were afraid the army would starve or run out of ammunition. But Grant fed his men from the farms through which he passed, and marched so fast that the Confederates did not know where he was. They kept sending parts of their army out to cut his supply line, but as he did not have any, these small forces ran into Grant's big one and were beaten, one after another.

The soldiers did not have to use many bullets, and although they had to march long and fast, they were having a wonderful time. They had chicken or turkey to eat almost every day and they knew they were winning.

At last Grant's men came up with the main army defending Vicksburg at the crossing of the Big Black River. Just as the Union army came up with the Confederates an officer arrived from Washington with an order saying that what Grant had done was too dangerous. He was to go back to the river. Grant stuck the order in his pocket and said nothing. The officer said: "Do you mean to say you will disobey this order?"

Grant only pointed to the bridge. Just at this moment the Union soldiers charged it with a hurrah and broke right through the Confederate line. This drove the Confederates back into Vicksburg. Since Grant now had the high bluffs on either side of the city, he could get all the supplies he wanted down the river merely by hauling them up the bluffs. But the Confederates could get no supplies from the country because of Grant's army all around the city, and the Union gunboats kept them from getting any from across the river. When the only thing left to eat in Vicksburg was mule meat, and people had to live in caves because shells had smashed all the houses, the town surrendered.

This was the second time Grant had taken a whole Confederate army. After this nobody dared to complain about him again, and people sent him boxes of cigars from all over the country. Vicksburg was even more important than Gettysburg. After it was taken ships could carry wheat from the West down the river and all the way to Europe, which was very useful, since there were few railroads. Also the Confederacy was cut in half and the armies fighting under Lee and other generals could no longer get men and supplies from across the great river.

THE ROCK OF CHICKAMAUGA
[*September 19–20, 1863*]

ROSECRANS' army started from Nashville in the spring of the same year that saw Lee marching to Gettysburg and Grant getting behind Vicksburg. Between him and Chattanooga were several rows of mountains, and the country is so poor it is called the "pine barrens." Campaigning there was difficult and slow, because all the supplies had to be carried in long trains of wagons, and as there were no paved roads they could not move fast.

Rosecrans would bring his army up to a mountain, the top of which was held by the Confederates, then hunt along it till he found a place where he could cross. Some of his men would be sent over to get behind the Confederates and they would have to retreat. There were no real battles, but the men had to march and climb all day, and when they tried to be comfortable around a campfire, someone would shoot at them from the dark trees.

All summer long this went on. Finally Bragg's Confederates were pushed back so far they had to give up Chattanooga. This was so serious for the Confederates that a large part of Lee's army was sent to help Bragg. This gave him more men than Rosecrans, so he turned to fight a battle in Chickamauga Valley. For a whole day the two long lines of men fired at each other from trees and clumps of bushes, and many were killed. That night both sides slept on the ground with their guns beside them.

Next morning the battle again and Rosecrans made a terrible mistake. He ordered one Union division to change its position without noticing in the thick woods that this would leave a hole in the Union line. The Confederates burst through the hole and attacked the Union line from the flank and rear. Two thirds of Rosecrans' army was driven away into Chattanooga with the flying troops. He telegraphed to Washington that everything was lost.

But it was not lost yet. On the left of the line was General "Old Pap" Thomas. He suddenly saw Confederates coming at him from all directions. He ordered his men back to a round hill called Horseshoe Ridge and told them to stand firm. All afternoon and until the moon came up after dark he rode along the lines. At last there were no more bullets. When the last attack came, Thomas' men charged against it with bayonets while the general fired a revolver. This put an end to the Confederate attacks and the army was saved. After this Thomas was always known as the "Rock of Chickamauga."

THE BATTLE ABOVE THE CLOUDS
[*November 23–25, 1863*]

THE CONFEDERATES now came up to the mountains around Chattanooga. They expected to shut the Union army in. But Lincoln made Grant commander of all the Union armies in the West and Grant hurried to Chattanooga with a corps and soon found a way of getting supplies to the army there. Next he gave command of the army to Thomas instead of Rosecrans. When the men heard that Thomas was their new commander, they broke ranks and cheered until he had to run away to hide the fact that he was blushing.

Now 15,000 men from the Army of the Potomac were placed under fighting Joe Hooker and sent to join Thomas. They crossed the country by railroad, which was very much harder to do than it would be today. The railroads did not run through most cities, so the men had to get off the train at one side of town, walk across, and take another train. There were no bridges across the great rivers, so temporary bridges had to be built on coal barges floating in the streams. In some places the tracks were farther apart than in others, so the tracks had to be torn up and relaid. All this was done so rapidly that Hooker's men reached Chattanooga a week after leaving Washington, going all the way round through Pittsburgh, Cincinnati, and Louisville. Nobody had ever heard of moving so many men such a distance so fast.

Now Grant was ready to fight a battle. The main Confederate position was along the top of Missionary Ridge, but out in front of it they had a strong post on Lookout Mountain, from which they could see everything the Union troops were doing. Just before daybreak Hooker's men began climbing Lookout Mountain. There was a heavy fog on the hills that morning and all the men in Chattanooga came out to watch anxiously as they saw the guns flashing through the mist. At last the first rays of the sun broke through to show a man standing on the highest rock, waving a flag. It was the Stars and Stripes and it showed Hooker had won.

Next day Grant sent most of his men against one end of Missionary Ridge, but they did not get far because the ground was so steep and rough. Grant ordered Thomas' men forward to take some shallow trenches at the bottom of the front of the ridge, thinking this might draw the Confederates' attention.

But when the Union soldiers had taken the trenches they found they could not stay there. The Confederates were firing on them from more trenches halfway up and from cannon at the top. Without anyone giving them orders, the soldiers suddenly began to cheer and climb. It was a wonderful charge up the slope of the mountain, with guns firing in their faces. In one place six men were killed carrying a flag, but no one let it touch the ground. In another a little wounded bugler boy sat on a rock, blowing "Charge!" till he fainted. Suddenly the Union soldiers were on top of the ridge, driving the Confederates right away before them. They captured many prisoners and all Bragg's guns, and the Confederates had to retreat in a hurry.

Part Three

THREE YEARS OF WAR

THE BATTLE OF CHATTANOOGA drove the Confederates out of Tennessee and they had lost the Mississippi River when Grant took Vicksburg. But these gains for the Union did not look very important on the map and hardly anyone knew how badly the Confederacy had been hurt. In 1864 a new President and Congress would be elected. Most people were tired of the war, and in New York there were terrible riots when more men were called to serve as soldiers. Unless the Union armies could really show they had a good chance of capturing all the Confederate armies and all the important cities, people would probably elect a new President who would make peace, leaving the Union broken into two countries. If this happened there would probably always be wars between them.

President Lincoln knew all this and was very anxious to see the war brought near an end before the elections. He called Grant to Washington and placed him in command of all the Union armies. Grant decided to stay with the Army of the Potomac, but brought Little Phil Sheridan with him to command the cavalry. He left General W. T. Sherman in command of the Army of the West at Chattanooga. Then he explained his plan to Lincoln.

Grant himself would follow Lee wherever he went, fighting him so hard he would not be able to spare a man to help out the Confederates in the West. Sherman would fight his way through the mountains to Atlanta, Georgia, the most important city in the South, then turn north to get behind Lee. When Lincoln heard the plan, he said: "I see. You intend to hold the leg while Sherman takes off the skin."

GRANT IN THE WILDERNESS
[April–September 1864]

LEE'S ARMY was on the south side of the Rappahannock, in the Wilderness where he had beaten Hooker. As soon as the ground was dry enough for guns and wagons Grant crossed and marched right into the woods. A battle began that lasted two whole days. The woods were full of long lines of smoke, and they were burning in some places. Hardly anyone could tell where he was. All the men could see were long lines of trenches and breastworks stretching away through the trees, with Confederates firing from behind them.

In this kind of war it was much easier for the men in the trenches, and after two days it was clear Grant could not break through. But instead of giving up and going back as the other Union generals had done, Grant moved sidewise, trying to get past Lee's army toward Richmond. Lee had less distance to go and got across Grant's path at Spotsylvania. Once more there was a battle lasting for several days across breastworks. In some places the soldiers on the two sides were so close that they shot and stabbed at each other across piles of logs. So many men were killed at Spotsylvania that it was called the "Bloody Angle."

All through May and June this kind of fighting went on. Grant's army would move sidewise and when it found the Confederates in its way there would be a battle. So many men were wounded in these battles that all the hospitals of Washington could not hold them. People at home felt downhearted and began calling Grant "the Butcher."

They did not understand what was really happening. Lee had not lost as many men as Grant, but he was losing more than he could afford, because the Confederacy could not replace those he lost. His army was wearing out. In the early part of the war Lee had beaten the Union generals by making quick marches around them and attacking them suddenly from the flank or behind. But Grant stayed so close to him and fought him so hard that he could not get away to make one of these marches. All he could do was build more trenches and forts to keep Grant from breaking through.

Finally Grant had moved sidewise so many times that he was besieging Petersburg, which is south of Richmond. The railroads that brought food and other supplies to Lee's army met at Petersburg. If Grant took the city, Lee would have to give up Richmond. But the forts around it were very strong. So Grant settled down to a siege of Petersburg. The men lived in huts behind the trenches, which grew deeper and wider every day. Guns fired all the time and anyone who stuck his head above the breastworks would probably be shot.

To most people it seemed as though Grant was not accomplishing much. But he was doing exactly what he had said he would do at the beginning of the campaign. He was keeping the Confederates so busy defending themselves that Lee could not think of anything else.

SHERMAN MOVES TOWARD ATLANTA
[Summer 1864]

GENERAL BRAGG had been so badly beaten at Chattanooga that his army was given to Joe Johnston. Facing him across lines of mountains was Sherman with the Union Army of the West. The soldiers called him "Uncle Billy" and liked

him because he slept on the ground instead of in a tent, and ate his food out of a tin can just as they did.

Sherman started toward Atlanta on the same day Grant entered the Wilderness. Along each ridge and river he came to, the Confederates had lines of trenches. Sherman moved up until the men on both sides were so close they could shoot at each other. But he always kept one corps ready to move around behind the Confederates. Once he sent this corps through a narrow pass in the mountains. Once he brought a lot of guns to the bank of a river, and made a great noise as though he intended to cross there, while more men slipped far up the stream and crossed very quietly.

There were hard battles all through this campaign. The Confederates held onto every position as long as they could to make Sherman use up his supplies. There was only one line of railroad reaching back to Chattanooga, and then to Ohio, and the Confederates burned the bridges and tore up the tracks as they retreated. They thought that someday Sherman would run out of food and bullets.

But Sherman's men were mostly farmers and lumbermen from the Northwest, used to making things for themselves. When they came to a swamp, they cut down trees and built a wooden road through it. They built bridges faster than the Confederates could burn them, even while the guns were shooting. They repaired the railroad so fast that the Confederates often heard the whistle of a new train behind the Union army. During this campaign Sherman's men had to march more than two hundred fifty miles, carrying heavy rifles and packs that held their food and ammunition and extra clothes. They let their beards grow very long, because it was too much trouble to carry extras like razors, and there was not much soap.

At last Johnston was driven back to the Chattahoochee River. President Davis grew annoyed with Johnston because he kept retreating instead of trying to drive Sherman away, and gave the army to General John B. Hood. He had only one leg and one arm, but he was known as a terrible fighter.

Sherman crossed the Chattahoochee River north of Atlanta and began to come down toward the city from two sides. But the maps used by the Union

51

generals were wrong and a big gap opened between two parts of the Union army. Hood thought this a fine chance and sent most of his own men out to attack part of the Union army under General Thomas. He hoped to break this part up and cut off the rest of the army.

But, as the Confederates had found before, it was not easy to break up an army under Thomas. He formed his men in little circles on the tops of some hills and rode from one to the other, placing guns and telling the men to stand fast. They stood fast so well that the Confederates lost a great many men and were driven back into Atlanta.

Now Sherman brought his army down around the north and east of Atlanta and his men dug trenches opposite the forts around the city. This gave Hood another chance. During the night he sent a large part of his army around the end of the Union trench line. As soon as it grew light, he attacked these trenches from behind. Other Confederates were to attack them from in front.

Almost any soldiers but "Uncle Billy" Sherman's men would have run away. But they did not think they could be beaten. When they were attacked from behind they jumped over the breastworks and fought in the other direction. Sherman brought some guns up to help them and the Confederate attack was broken. Just then the Confederates who were to attack the trenches in front arrived. They were now behind Sherman's men, but the Union soldiers simply jumped over the breastworks again. This attack, too, was beaten off and the Confederates were driven into Atlanta.

Hood had lost so many men in these attacks that, like Lee in Virginia, he could not afford to attack any more. But he had plenty to hold the forts around Atlanta. The battles turned into a siege, like the one at Petersburg.

THE COMING OF THE ELECTIONS
[Summer 1864]

BOTH Grant and Sherman knew they were wearing the Confederate armies out, but most people back home in the North did not understand this. They kept hearing of battles and men being killed or wounded, but Richmond and Petersburg held out, and so did Atlanta, and the Confederacy looked almost as strong as ever.

Many people were so tired of the war that they were willing to let the Union go to pieces if they could only have peace. They held a big convention in Chicago and nominated General McClellan against Lincoln for President. They said: "The war is a failure."

Even some of those on Lincoln's side thought so too. They did not see how the Confederacy could ever be beaten. Lincoln himself thought there were so many of these that, he told close friends, he did not believe he could be re-elected.

EARLY AND SHERIDAN
[*July–September 1864*]

GENERAL LEE knew how badly his army was wearing out. He decided he would have to do something to make Grant let go at Petersburg. He remembered how frightened everyone in the North had been when Stonewall Jackson marched down the Shenandoah Valley in 1862, and how Lincoln had sent troops from everywhere after him. So Lee sent General Jubal Early into the Valley with a small army. Even if this did not make Lincoln call back part of Grant's men, it might make people in the North still more discouraged and tired of the war.

Early quickly beat the small Union army in the Valley, crossed the Potomac, and came down toward Washington, so close he could see the Capitol. Lincoln went out to the forts, and bullets whistled around him until someone pulled him down. Of course Early did not have enough men to try to take Washington, but the fact he was there made people in the North still more depressed. Then Early marched into Pennsylvania and burned the town of Chambersburg.

This annoyed Grant. He sent troops from several different places into the Shenandoah Valley to make a new army and placed Little Phil Sheridan in command of it. Sheridan waited until his men got to know him and then marched against Early at Winchester. There was a hard battle in open fields and around little hills. But toward evening some of Sheridan's cavalry came down on the end of Early's line. The Confederates gave way and began to run through the twilight.

Early got his men together at Fisher's Hill three days later. There he dug trenches across the top of a ridge, with mountains at both ends of his line. Sheridan's men could not climb the hill against the guns and Early's trenches. But Little Phil sent part of his men around one of the mountains at the end of Early's line. They moved forward slowly through the trees, with cloth wrapped around their guns to keep them from catching the sunlight. Just at twilight they unwrapped the cloths and charged. When Sheridan heard their bugles he ordered the rest of the army forward, right up the hill. Every time anyone asked him anything, he would shout: "Forward, everything!" and swing his hat. The Confederates were taken from two sides at once and driven far up the Valley.

SHERMAN AT ATLANTA
[August–September 1864]

THESE two splendid victories made people in the North feel better, especially since they had taken place so soon after Early had approached Washington. Right on their heels came a still more important piece of news. Sherman had taken Atlanta!

Sherman knew that the election probably depended on what he did there. In the long run he could take the city by siege, but this would be too late to do any good. So he took most of his men out of the trenches and started marching fast around the city against the railroads from the south by which Hood's army got supplies. This was dangerous, because he could not even take along wagons to carry his own supplies, but he thought the men could live on fresh green corn from the fields for long enough to make the campaign a success.

In Atlanta, when they found the Union soldiers gone from the trenches, they thought Sherman must have given up and was going back to Tennessee. A great ball was held to celebrate the victory. But in the middle of the ball the sound of Sherman's cannon came booming from the south. The officers had to stop dancing and hurry to join their troops. The Confederates tried to stop Sherman before he got across the railroad line, but he beat them in a battle. and after that there was nothing to do but give up the city.

The news from Sheridan and Sherman was so good that in two of the state elections, which were held early, Congressmen in favor of Lincoln were chosen. There was also more good news.

FARRAGUT AT MOBILE BAY
[August 1864]

MOBILE, Alabama, was one of the last big cities still held by the Confederates. At the entrance to the bay on which it stands were two strong forts. Inside the bay the Confederates had a small fleet of wooden ships and a big ironclad ram. the *Tennessee*. Old Admiral Farragut blockaded the bay for a long time with several wooden ships. When the navy sent him four monitors, Farragut decided to force his way past the forts and fight the ram.

Between the forts was a line of floating torpedoes, or mines. The ships steamed into the gap between the forts, both sides fighting furiously, just as when Farragut made his way up the Mississippi to New Orleans. At this moment a torpedo went off under the monitor *Tecumseh* and she sank in less than two minutes. The other ships hesitated as though they meant to turn back, with cannon balls striking them all the time, and someone shouted: "Torpedoes! Torpedoes!" Standing in the rigging of his flagship, old Admiral Farragut cried: "Damn the torpedoes! Full speed ahead!" The line of ships straightened out behind him and broke into the bay.

Now the *Tennessee* attacked the Union fleet. The Union wooden ships tried to ram her, but they only damaged their own prows and her guns tore great holes in their sides. But she could not hurt the monitors, and shot from their big guns broke her armor and carried away her steering gear. The *Tennessee* had to surrender, and as the forts could no longer get supplies across the bay, they soon surrendered too.

SHERIDAN'S RIDE
[*October 19, 1864*]

AFTER Sheridan had beaten Early at Fisher's Hill he followed the Confederates up the Shenandoah Valley, burning all the crops and barns, so that Lee's army could no longer obtain food from there. On the way back his army camped at Cedar Creek, while Sheridan rode to Winchester to talk to the Secretary of War. During the night Early, with some new troops from Lee's army, marched fast and very quietly after Sheridan. At daybreak they attacked the Union camp. Many of the men in it were still asleep. They were surprised and two thirds of them had no chance to do anything but run away down the road.

Sheridan heard the sound of the guns in the distance just as he finished breakfast. As he got on his big black horse, Rienzi, and started to ride toward the army, he met little groups of men running away. Little Phil stood in his stirrups and shouted: "Turn, boys, turn! We're going back!" When the men saw who it was, they shouted: "Sheridan!" and turned around to follow him. By the time he and the big black horse reached the battlefield, all the men who had run away in the morning were behind him.

He found part of the army holding out on a hill. The men he brought with him formed into line under any officers they saw. Then Sheridan ordered a charge with more than two hundred bugles blowing "Rally." The Confederates were carried right away before that charge. Early's army lost many prisoners and all its guns and was broken up.

All over the North people fired salutes and held parades as though it were the Fourth of July in celebration of this great victory. On top of Sheridan's other battles and Sherman taking Atlanta and Farragut winning at Mobile, anyone could see that the war was not a failure. They voted for Lincoln instead of the opponents who said it was, and he was easily re-elected.

THE MARCH TO THE SEA
[*Autumn 1864*]

HOOD and his army turned away west after Sherman took Atlanta, and started toward Tennessee. This left Sherman puzzled. He could not follow Hood without going back where he started from, and this would not do much to win the war.

Sherman finally decided to cut loose from everything and march across Georgia to the sea. His men would live off the country during the march. When they reached the coast they could be supplied from ships and he would turn north to get behind Lee's army. He sent General Thomas back to Nashville with part of his men to keep Hood from going north. Then he burned Atlanta to keep the Confederates from using its shops and factories, and set out.

Even Lincoln and Grant were worried about what would happen to Sherman in a country where everyone was against him, but they need not have been. The Confederates tried to gather troops to stop him, but they got so few that his men only shouted: "We're Billy Sherman's boys. You better git!" and the Confederates would run away. All across Georgia, Sherman's men tore up the railroads and burned the bridges for a space sixty miles wide. They burned up the storehouses and ate all the food in the country. It was more like a picnic than war, though it was very hard on the people of Georgia. On Christmas Day Sherman captured Savannah and then turned north.

This march through Georgia was very important. It cut the Confederacy in half for a second time, just as the capture of the Mississippi had before. After it, trains could no longer cross Georgia to bring food and supplies from the other Southern states to Lee's army at Richmond. Not even mail from Richmond could be sent across the state. This meant that the Confederate government had lost everything but the states of Virginia and North and South Carolina. Everyone could see now that the Union was really winning the war.

THOMAS TRAPS HOOD
[December 1864]

ON HIS WAY north toward Nashville, Hood found part of Thomas' men behind some log breastworks at Franklin, Tennessee. The Confederates attacked fiercely in the twilight, but many of the Union soldiers had the new repeating rifles that would fire seven shots without reloading. They said afterward that it made it look as though the ground was paved with fire. The attack was not a success and the Confederates lost a great many men, but they followed the Union army to Nashville and dug trenches in front of the city.

General Grant was very anxious for Thomas to attack Hood, to keep him from slipping away. He kept sending Thomas telegrams telling him to attack, and finally grew so impatient that he sent another general to replace Thomas. Before the other general could arrive, Thomas had finished his preparations and did attack.

Part of his men were laborers, not real soldiers at all, but they were dressed in blue uniforms and sent to make a big noise opposite one wing of Hood's army. Then Thomas attacked Hood's other wing with all his men. The Confederates were driven from their trenches and back to a line of hills. The next morning Thomas sent his foot soldiers against these hills while the cavalry went around behind. When they were attacked from both sides the Confederates broke. That was the end of Hood's army. Those who were not captured simply scattered through the country. A big Union army of cavalry marched all through Alabama and Mississippi and captured everything there was to capture. Except for a small army that still held out in Texas, the war in the West was over.

SHERMAN IN THE CAROLINAS
[January–March 1865]

AFTER he took Savannah, Sherman began marching north through South Carolina. There were no roads and no bridges. The country is crossed by wide rivers, running through swamps that are often seven or eight miles across. It seemed impossible that an army with all its guns and baggage could move through such country. But Sherman's men, who had walked and fought all that distance from Minnesota and Wisconsin and Michigan, were not going to be stopped now. They chopped down the trees to make roads and bridges. When they came to a river some of them would swim across to drive away any Confederates on the other side, while the rest chopped and built. In one place they built fifteen long bridges in a single day.

Many fine homes were burned, and when Sherman's men came to a

plantation, the Negro slaves usually ran away to follow, because they would be free. The Confederates tried hard to get men together to stop Sherman, but there were too many of Uncle Billy's boys and they had too many guns. Soon they had crossed South Carolina and were marching into North Carolina.

LEE'S LAST TRY
[*March 25–April 1, 1865*]

LEE knew that if he let Sherman come up behind him he would be trapped. He planned to break through Grant's line of forts at Petersburg and burn up his storehouses. This would keep Grant's army from moving. Then Lee would slip away from Richmond and join the troops in North Carolina to beat Sherman.

Lee's men attacked Fort Stedman, east of Petersburg, at half past four on a dark morning. The Confederates captured this fort, but they could go no farther. Union troops rallied around from every direction, and the Confederates were killed or driven back.

As soon as Grant heard of this he understood exactly what Lee was trying to do. He gave Little Phil Sheridan a corps of infantry and 15,000 cavalry and sent him to get across the roads leading west out of Petersburg. This would shut Lee in so closely he would have to give up Richmond.

Lee sent a large force of his own men to stop Sheridan, under General Pickett, who led the famous charge at Gettysburg. At first Pickett drove part of Sheridan's men back, but more and more Union troops came up, and Pickett was driven back to a line of trenches around Five Forks. Sheridan charged these trenches, leading the charge himself on his big black horse, waving a flag. Nearly all Pickett's little army was lost.

THE FINAL MARCH
[April 2–9, 1865]

WHEN this news came President Lincoln went down to join the army because everyone could see that the Confederacy was nearly finished. Grant's men attacked the forts at Petersburg and broke into the city. On a Sunday morning Lee called President Davis out of church and told him he would have to give up Richmond and try to get away to the mountains.

As Lee's army turned west, Sheridan kept striking at it with his cavalry. Every time Lee's men stopped to drive Sheridan off, the Union infantry corps would gain along roads farther south. Lee's men were tired and badly outnumbered and had little to eat. Many of them were captured.

Finally they reached Appomattox Court House, where they found a line of Union cavalry right across the road. The Confederates got ready to drive the cavalry off, but as they did so it moved to one side without fighting. Behind them were long lines of Union infantry with many cannon. Lee's army was trapped. There was no direction it could go.

Lee sent a messenger with a white flag to Grant. The two generals met at the house of a Mr. McLean. Lee was in his best uniform, but Grant had been marching so fast that the only thing he had to wear was an old private's coat. They talked for a few minutes, then Grant wrote out terms for the surrender of Lee's army and Lee signed them. He was pleased when he saw that Grant had written down that any man who had a horse should be allowed to take it home for farm work.

When the other Confederate generals heard Lee had surrendered, they surrendered too, and the Civil War was over.

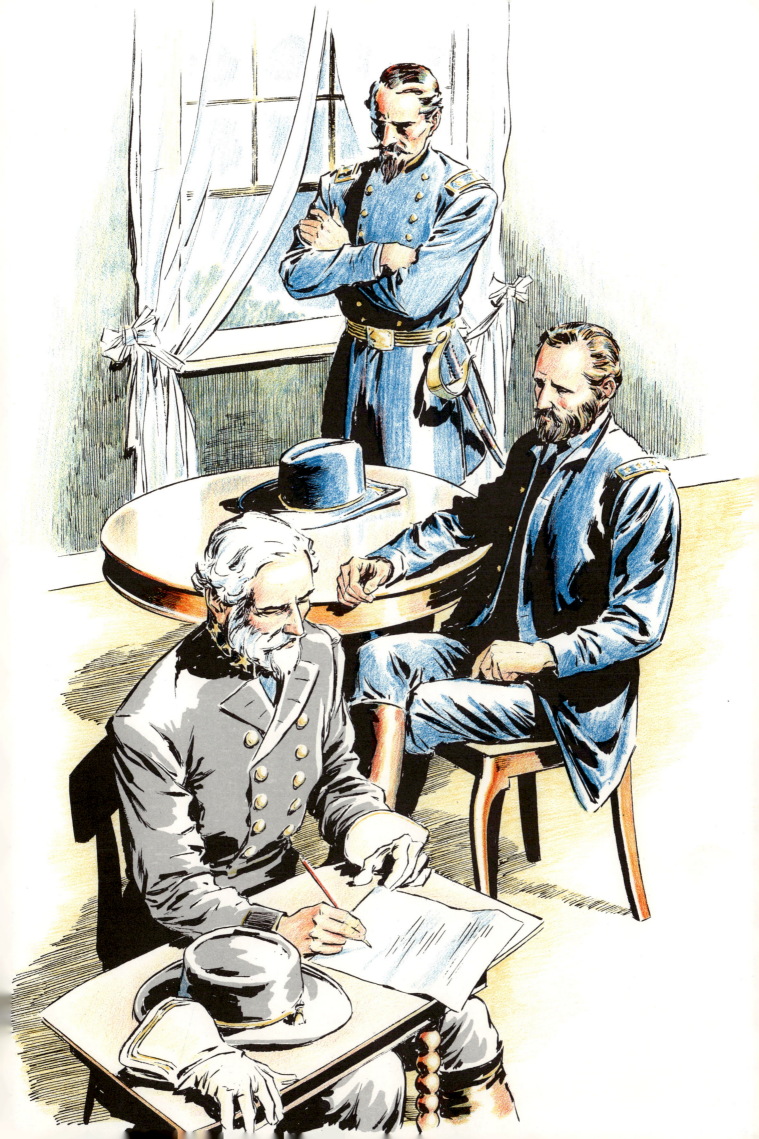

c